MARK

THE SUFFERING SERVANT

10 Publishing
a division of 10 of those.com

MARK: The Suffering Servant
Copyright © 2012 Jeremy McQuoid

Published 2012

Published by 10Publishing, a division of 10ofthose.com
Unit 19 Common Bank Industrial Estate, Ackhurst Road, Chorley, PR7 1NH
Email: info@10ofthose.com
Website: www.10ofthose.com

British Library Cataloguing in Publication Data.
A catalogue record for this book is available from the British Library.

ISBN: 978-1-906173-55-5

Cover Design and Typeset by: Diane Bainbridge
Printed by: www.printbridge.co.uk

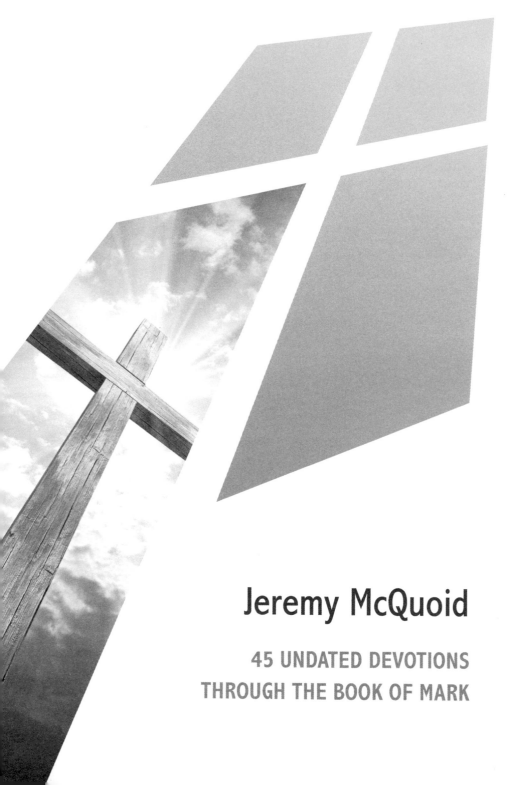

Jeremy McQuoid

45 UNDATED DEVOTIONS
THROUGH THE BOOK OF MARK

INTRODUCTION

Until the early 1900s, not many people bothered with Mark's Gospel. Why would you? It seemed the poor relation of the much longer Gospels of Matthew and Luke, which contained most of Mark's stories, and so much more besides. But interest in Mark suddenly sparked into life when scholars began to realize that Mark was the first Gospel written. It was the original Gospel.

Matthew and Luke based their longer Gospels on Mark, and quoted from it, at times almost word for word. That is how revered Mark's Gospel was. Mark is also special precisely because it is shorter than the others. It was written to a group of suffering Christians, probably in Rome, who were facing execution, and had no time for theological intricacies. They needed to know the most essential parts of the Gospel, without getting lost in theological jargon.

Who is Jesus, and why is He worth dying for? Mark even does away with any reference to Jesus' birth, so he can focus on the most essential stories that convey the meaning and power of Jesus' life, death and resurrection. He presents Jesus as a gripping hero figure who heals, confronts, exorcizes and resurrects, all at breakneck speed (Mark's favourite linking word between stories is 'immediately').

One third of the Gospel is devoted to the week of Jesus' death. Mark's message is clear – the all-conquering Son of God is also God's 'suffering servant', and the true meaning of His life revolves around a cross, three hours of darkness and an empty tomb.

The other intriguing attraction of Mark's Gospel is that many of the eyewitness accounts probably come from Peter, who got closer to Jesus than anyone. There are clear pointers to eyewitness testimony – the greenness of the grass at the feeding of the 5,000, the vividness of the transfiguration, the fact that the actual words of Jesus in Aramaic are preserved at key points in the text. We know that Mark was with Peter towards the end of Peter's life, and no one else would have dared write about Peter's abject failure at Jesus' trial, apart from the great apostle himself. So much of this Gospel carries Peter's stamp – it is about failing disciples who can barely grasp who Jesus is, and who stumble as they try to follow Him. It's a gospel for ordinary men and women.

So here is the original gospel of Jesus, written from the vivid perspective of His closest friend. The unadorned, 'no frills', pure Gospel of Jesus, raw and ready to change your life.

Jeremy McQuoid

Mark has a very 'cut-to-the-chase' style. While Matthew and Luke begin their Gospels with stories of Jesus' birth and elaborate family trees, Mark has no time for such intricacies. He tells us right away what his message is about 'The beginning of the gospel about Jesus Christ, the Son of God.'

The sprinter Linford Christie spoke about starting a race on the 'b' of 'bang'. That is the urgency that sparks from Mark's quill. He is desperate to tell people the message of Jesus. And in this opening verse he uses three phrases that are key to that message:

1. Gospel – the word means 'good news'. It is often linked with the verb 'preach' in the New Testament. It pictures a town crier announcing the edict of the king. This gospel is God's authoritative announcement to the world. It can only be 'good news' however, if people are clear about the bad news that precedes it. God is angry at our sin (Rom. 1:18–20), but has chosen, out of sheer love, to give us Jesus as a 'propitiation' or 'anger-bearing sacrifice' (see Rom. 3:25).

2. Christ – Jesus did not come into our world in a vacuum. He was the fulfilment of centuries of prophecy that the 'Christ' (in Hebrew 'the Messiah'), would come to save God's people from their sin. The word 'messiah' means 'anointed one' and refers to the anointing of kings in Israel who were set apart for the task of kingship by God. Jesus is God's anointed king, set apart for His kingly task – dying on a cross to bring salvation to a lost world.

3. Son of God – Mark is actually more interested in the title 'Son of God' than he is in the title 'Christ' (Matthew's favourite theme). In the first half of the gospel, Mark presents Jesus as the supernatural healer who casts out demons, heals the sick, calms storms, and opposes the Pharisees all at breakneck speed, to prove that He is the Son of God – full of power and authority.

Notice Mark does not introduce the gospel as a set of propositions we need to believe, but as a person we need to believe on (John 3:16) – 'Jesus Christ, the Son of God', whom we need to love, honour and obey. Ultimately, the gospel is very personal. It is not just a message to the world; it is a personal relationship with a loving, powerful Saviour. Paul summed it up by calling Jesus 'the Son of God, *who loved me and gave himself for me*' (Gal. 2:20).

REFLECTION

Do you love Jesus? Are you convinced of Jesus' love for you? How desperate are you to tell others about Him?

Why did John the Baptist conduct his entire ministry in the desert? Surely that wasn't the best place for God to send him. Why didn't he set up a podium in Jerusalem Main Street on a Saturday afternoon, or better still the Temple with all the crowds milling around? Why do we have this strange scenario where, 'The whole Judean countryside and all the people of Jerusalem *went out to him*' (v. 5), in a 110-degree desert?

Could it be that God wanted to encourage the people away from the hustle and bustle of their daily city lives, to the austere quiet of the desert, so they could really listen to Him? Emails and demanding jobs and screaming children and 24-hour cities make quiet spaces hard to find. But you need quiet to hear from God, as Elijah learned from the 'still small voice' (1 Kgs. 19:12, KJV). God wanted to prepare Israel for the good news of Christ's coming, but in a context where they were ready to listen to Him.

And perhaps the barrenness and austerity of a desert matched John's austere message. He was not calling people to a razzmatazz revival, but to a 'baptism of repentance for the forgiveness of sins' (v. 4). If people were going to be truly ready for Jesus, they needed to strip their own lives bare of pride, apathy and greed, like a desert is stripped bare of any form of earth's comforts.

That's what baptism pictures. We 'died with Christ' through baptism (see Rom. 6:3). Baptism represents the death of my 'old' self, so that my 'new self' in Christ – His love, His sacrificial spirit, His absolute obedience to His Father – can take its place. New life can only take root when the old life is dead and buried. As believers we need to confess our sins each morning to God and ask Him to strip away all that hinders His Spirit working through us to produce Christ-likeness.

Crucifying the flesh calls for discipline, stripping away the excesses in our life, and a barren desert is a great visual reminder of that process. That is how we 'Prepare the way for the Lord' (v. 3) in our own hearts.

REFLECTION

Where can you find quiet so that you can hear God's voice? What needs to be stripped away from your life to make it ready for Jesus?

Simon and Garfunkel used to sing about 'The Sound of Silence'. And before we race on with Jesus' public ministry, it is worth meditating on 'Jesus – the silent years'. Mark says absolutely nothing about the first thirty years of Jesus' life. He simply begins 'At that time [when he's about 30 years old] Jesus came from Nazareth in Galilee' (v. 9).

The longer gospels don't add much either. Matthew says a little about His birth, and Luke adds a wonderful story about Jesus the 12 year old confounding the Bible scholars in the Temple with His great learning. But other than that, the gospels are deafeningly silent about Jesus' early years.

The snippet Mark gives us, 'Nazareth in Galilee', suggests Jesus was brought up in modest seclusion. Nazareth was a tiny town which archaeologists have struggled to find (population 120 in Jesus' day), and so despised by Jews that Nathaniel asked, 'Can anything good come from there?' (John 1:46). Jewish sophisticates lived in the south, near Jerusalem where the pulse of Israel's national life was measured. But Nazareth? It was obscure even by backward Galilee standards!

Jesus lived for thirty years in a quiet, dusty town, where nothing much ever happened, under the authority of His working-class parents. Luke's 'Jesus in the Temple' story ends with Jesus going home and being 'subject' (Luke 2:51, KJV) to His parents again, and He probably attended His father's funeral in His teenage years. Joseph is not in the picture by the time Jesus goes public.

But sometimes silence is striking. Jesus, in His first thirty years, represents us in the mundane things of life. He obeyed His parents, was brought up in a dull little town. Nothing is known about Him, not even if He was longing for adventure, like Luke Skywalker as a farm boy longing to be involved in intergalactic *Star Wars*.

None of us can escape the mundane in life. Hanging out the clothes, taxi-ing the children, filling out endless paperwork, stacking the chairs on a Sunday. We spend more time sleeping than we do in church. 'Jesus – the silent years' reminds us that He lived through all our dreary Mondays, all our 'what's-life-all-about' sighs, and He did it in obedience to His Father. In 'Jesus – the silent years', we hear the echoes of Paul – 'whatever you do [even if what you do isn't very thrilling], do it all for the glory of God' (1 Cor. 10:31).

REFLECTION

How can you glorify God in the mundane responsibilities of life? Think about work, church service, everyday activities such as shopping, cooking, walking the dog, visiting friends, taking care of children, elderly parents and so on.

Neil Armstrong's words as he first stepped onto the surface of the moon, have been immortalized – 'That's one small step for man, one giant leap for mankind.' Clearly the Apollo 11 astronauts saw their mission as, in some sense, for the whole of humanity.

So did Jesus at His baptism. As Christ stepped into the River Jordan He was deliberately accepting God's mission as a representative of all humanity. He represents us

1. In the decision He makes. It was a bold move to come out of the 'safety' of Nazareth life into the cauldron of public preaching, healing and conflict. Jesus calls all of us out of 'safe' living, into the firing line. Is our testimony for Christ bold and visible enough to make us unpopular? Is God calling you to step out of the shadows and take on a challenging ministry?

2. In the sin He carries. Why was Jesus baptized? Baptism was about repentance, but Jesus had nothing to repent of. Yet Jesus chose to be baptized to identify Himself with sinners. One day He would be clothed in our sins, becoming our substitute on the cross. He later referred to the cross as His 'baptism'. Peter says, 'He himself bore our sins in his body on the tree' (1 Pet. 2:24).

3. In the approval He receives. As Jesus stepped out of the water, the heavens opened and God affirmed, 'You are My beloved Son' (NKJV). Jesus the man probably needed that affirmation, and He got it before He had ever done anything eye-catching in public ministry. God calls you and me His 'beloved sons'. If we trust in Jesus, we have that status regardless of whether or not we do anything that pleases the Father (see Rom. 8:17).

4. In the temptations He faces. In the Greek, the word for 'sent' is 'throw', so the Spirit literally 'throws' Jesus into the desert. For the devil this was a chance to tempt, but for God it was the opportunity to prove His Son's obedience. God sometimes throws us into fiery trials to prove that our faith is worth more than gold (see 1 Pet. 1:6,7).

REFLECTION

Do you need to come out of the shadows in your Christian life? In what area? Do you realize that you are God's beloved son/ daughter in Christ, and that you are accepted and unconditionally loved by Him?

Did your alarm clock wake you up this morning? My alarm has this high-pitched, repetitive shriek, but I am usually so comatose I need to take that kind of drastic measure to get going in the morning.

Jesus did not ease His way gently into Galilean hearts. He set off a shrill alarm to awaken a spiritually decadent culture. It had been over four hundred years since Israel heard a prophetic voice, but suddenly John the Baptist's straight-talking ministry was followed by Jesus' urgent message, 'The time has come...The kingdom of God is near. Repent and believe the good news!' (v. 15)

There is an urgency in following Christ. God has not revealed to us the day of Christ's return, nor the hour of our own demise (they could be any moment), and we live in a decadent world that needs to hear the gospel today! Have you lost your sense of urgency as a follower of Jesus?

Jesus' call is not only urgent, it is a call to total allegiance. Mark's brevity of words only highlights this truth. '"Come, follow me," Jesus said, "and I will make you fishers of men." At once they left their nets and followed him' (vv. 17,18). In case the radical nature of the way they abandoned their nets had not hit home, when Jesus calls James and John, Mark added the caveat, 'they left their father Zebedee in the boat with the hired men and followed [Jesus]' (v. 20).

The fishing industry was the livelihood of Galileans for generations, passed on from father to son. How extraordinary then that these men left the family business and close family ties to pursue Christ! But discipleship in Mark is always radical. Are you a more mellow disciple, dipping your toe into lukewarm discipleship, and secretly wondering why others get so passionate about Christ?

The gospel demands radical discipleship. Praying until we weep, witnessing until we are scorned, immersing ourselves in the Word, devoting ourselves to the church Jesus died to win. Half-heartedness has no place in a church built on the broken body of Christ. Jim Elliot, the martyred missionary to Ecuador, once wrote in his journal, 'Make me thy fuel, flame of God.'

Do you need a wake-up call? 'The time has come...'

Authority has more or less lost its authority in the twenty-first-century West. Our culture worships human rights and balks at anyone who suggests they have authority over us. If you doubt that, listen in to any radio talk show, note how the media talks about the government, or simply eavesdrop on a chat between church members about 'the elders'.

Jesus was always going to set the cat among the pigeons in Israel because 'he taught them as one who had authority' (v. 22). He did not quote other great teachers, as even the most eminent Jewish rabbis did. He usually quoted Himself – 'you have heard it said, but I say...' as though His own word was equal to God's.

And He doesn't just speak with authority, He demonstrates it by casting out demons: '"Be quiet!" said Jesus sternly. "Come out of him!"' (v. 25) He commands dark forces, and they obey, often with trembling. All of which leaves the people wondering, 'Who is more frightening – the demons, or the one who has just cast them out?'

When He gets to Peter's mother-in-law, He does not even say anything – 'he went to her, took her hand and helped her up. The fever left her...' (v. 31). How lovely it is that Jesus' power, which is frightening enough to make demons tremble, is also 'homely' enough to make a mother-in-law get up and prepare the tea.

'Who is this Jesus?' is the question Mark wants us to keep asking throughout his gospel. Should I love Him because He makes sick people well, or should I fear Him because He has untold power even over dark realms that I barely understand?

'A bit of both' is where Mark wants us to get to. Mark wants us to love our compassionate healer, who cares about our dearest loved ones, but he also wants us to fear, in a healthy way, the one who will crush Satan's head. We hear a lot in our churches about 'loving' Christ, often through sentimental worship songs. There is nothing wrong with that, except that we may lose a balanced perspective on our glorious Lord Jesus Christ. Proverbs reminds us that 'the fear of the LORD is the beginning of wisdom' (Prov. 9:10).

C.S. Lewis was right to depict Christ as the lion, Aslan, in his Narnia novels. A lion to whom even little children can talk, but also a lion who roars...

REFLECTION

Do you 'fear' Christ as much as you love Him? Who in your circle of family or friends needs His 'healing' right now?

It is a trait of human nature to look for an inspiring leader, a pop star or a sporting legend to set our pulses racing. And Christ was threatening to become just that to the peasant Galileans: 'The whole town gathered at the door' (v. 33) to bring their sick and demon-possessed for His touch. We will find throughout Mark's fast-paced action that Jesus' ministry is regularly overcrowded and hemmed in, and He has to go without food, such is the clamour that His miracle-working creates.

So in that context, notice Jesus' warning to the demons – 'he would not let the demons speak because they knew who he was' (v. 34). Would it not be great publicity for Jesus to have demons proclaim Him as the Son of God? Well, not in Jesus' mind.

Israel under Roman rule was a ferment of messianic expectation. The Messiah would come and free Israel from its Roman bondage and usher in a glorious new age, and Jesus is just the kind of miracle-working, charismatic leader the crowds were yearning for. But Jesus is wary of the clamour.

He has not come to heal, but to die, and build a spiritual, rather than a political, kingdom on the foundation of His own sacrifice for sin. So He commands the demons to be quiet about His true messianic status, for fear the people might get the wrong idea about what kind of Messiah He will be.

Then, when Simon (Peter) comes looking for Jesus, because the crowds are demanding His miracles, Jesus replies, 'Let us go somewhere else... so I can preach... That is why I have come' (v. 38). The 'narrow road' for Christ would not be satisfying the demands of a populist uprising, but preaching a kingdom built on humility, self-denial and death.

It would have been so easy for Christ to take the 'popular' road, as Satan tempted Him. But He shuns the clamour to blaze a different trail, which would reach its climax on a cross. And we face the same challenge in a myriad of ways all the time. Do I take the 'populist' route, in my social life at work, the way I go about climbing the career ladder, or in my relationships with friends and family? Or do I follow Christ? We constantly face the choice between popularity, acceptance, even acclaim, and true discipleship.

REFLECTION

In what areas of your life does following Jesus clash with popular expectation? Are you a good 'publicist' for Christ?

Remember pictures of Princess Diana touching an AIDS patient shocking the world? International AIDS agencies claimed that the touch of a princess, sent in news bulletins across the globe, achieved more for our understanding of AIDS sufferers than 100 ad campaigns could have ever done.

Leprosy victims have had to endure similar scars to AIDS sufferers. Lepers, in Jesus' day, were the 'untouchables' in society. They carried bells which they had to ring when anyone came within 50 yards of them, for fear that unwary passers-by may get contaminated. And they were excluded from synagogue worship – social and spiritual outcasts.

So you can sense both the emotion and the boldness of the leper, coming to Jesus on his knees, and 'begging' Him, 'If you are willing, you can make me clean' (v. 40). What we recognize less readily is how similar the leper's physical state is to our spiritual state outside of Christ.

Without Christ, we are spiritually 'unclean' to a God whose burning moral purity is appalled by every stain of sin. Our souls are oozing with the decay of sin in a way we barely understand, because we have little awareness of absolute, white-hot holiness.

As Isaiah discovered, God is not just 'holy' like the angels, or even 'holy, holy'. He is 'Holy, holy, holy', the sum of all perfections, and when we see our sin in the glare of His glory, even the best of us, such as Isaiah, must fall on our faces like unclean lepers, in despair (see Isa. 6:1–5).

But this leper acknowledges his helpless state, falls on his knees crying out for mercy, and believes by faith that Christ has the power to heal. What a picture of true 'broken spirit' repentance. It is the 'poor in spirit' who enter 'the kingdom of heaven' (Matt. 5:3). And what power in the simple phrase 'Jesus reached out his hand and touched the man' (v. 41).

Today, Jesus is still waiting to touch the lives of all who come to Him with humility, acknowledging their sin in the light of His glory. Christian salvation is about God pouring out His mercy on people who recognize their wretchedness. As Wesley wrote in his great hymn, ''Tis mercy all! Let earth adore, Let angel minds inquire no more.' ('And Can It Be', Charles Wesley, 1707–88)

Are you still excited about the mercy of God in your life?

REFLECTION

How thankful are you for your salvation? How do thoughts of God's holiness affect your daily conduct?

I used to love the 'Spaghetti Westerns' of Sergio Leone, where Clint Eastwood, 'The Man with No Name', would ride into dusty towns, and upset the oppressive power structures. Jesus does much the same in this next section of Mark, only without bullets or bloodshed.

Mark gathers together a series of five stories (2:1–3:6) based around the town of Capernaum, which was really 'home' for Jesus, but a place where 'a prophet was without honour' (see Mark 6:4). Each of these stories contains a conflict with religious leaders, the power brokers of their day. Jesus was exposing the staleness of religion based on human rules and rituals, and ushering in the 'new wine' of a grace-based, faith-driven, living relationship with God – the kind of relationship God had always wanted with His people.

The first story begins with a healing miracle where four people show remarkable tenacity in lowering their paralyzed friend through a roof in search of Jesus' healing touch (v. 4). It makes me question how much tenacity I show in bringing people to Christ. Faith is not merely a passive belief in doctrinal facts, but an active tenacity based on the promise of God's Word (note how 'active' Heb. 11 faith is).

But an unexpected twist is brought to the story when Jesus dares to forgive the paralytic's sins: 'Why does this fellow talk like that? He's blaspheming! Who can forgive sins but God alone?' (v. 7) The religionists found it inconceivable that the authoritative, gracious, life-giving rabbi may indeed be God.

That prompts Jesus to raise the issue of 'authority' again (v. 10), and the paralytic rising from his mat and walking, to everyone's astonishment, is now not merely a sign of Jesus' healing power, but of His divine right to forgive the sins of any who come to Him with tenacious faith.

Jesus calls Himself the 'Son of Man', His favourite title in Mark. The title comes from Daniel 7 where the 'Ancient of Days' gives the Son of Man 'authority' (there's the word again) over the nations of the world (Dan. 7:13,14). Notice, Jesus' priority as He exercises His 'Son of Man' authority is to forgive sins, not to heal bodies. He loves to do both, of course, but every healed body would die again, while those whose sins are forgiven receive the gift of eternal life (John 3:16). May we learn not to value the health of our bodies over the wellbeing of our souls (3 John 2)!

REFLECTION

*Is your faith tenacious?
Do you spend more time
on your body or your soul?*

The 1904 Welsh revival, where 100,000 souls were converted in a year, police stations were closed because of a lack of crime, and town drunks were found kneeling in chapels at 3 a.m., began, like so many of God's great works, in unexpected places. God bypassed the trained clergy, and used an uneducated miner's son in his mid-twenties named Evan Roberts, who longed for deeper fellowship with God, was filled with Holy Spirit power, and began a dynamic preaching campaign.

When Jesus chose His disciples, He seemed to skip over the likely candidates, the graduates of Pharisee school, and instead called fishermen (1:14–20), and now a tax collector (v. 14) to His band. God's grace seems to come most alive in those who know they can make no claim on it.

What was particularly irksome to the Pharisees was the sheer joy Jesus took, not only in calling sinners to be His disciples, but in eating with them. We underestimate the power of table fellowship. Who you have dinner with, the kind of company you keep, says much about who you are. Jesus loved to eat with 'sinners'. He still does, as millions of sinners gather round bread and wine every week.

There is something scandalous about grace, isn't there? We are brought up to believe that 'you get what you pay for,' hard work earns its rewards. But God's grace rips up the merit system of human attainment and forgives, and eats with, and befriends rebels who find it impossible to work their way into God's good books.

The gospel is all about the kind of grace that calls a tax collector from his deceitful practices, and entices him to lose his life for the kingdom of God. God used Abraham the wife swapper, Moses the murderer, David the adulterer, Peter the denier, Paul the terrorist, and yes, Matthew the tax collector – the kind of men who should have been in prison, but ended up being the most effective ambassadors for the power of saving grace.

Amazing grace! Don't ever lose its sweet rhythms in your heart.

REFLECTION

Are you still amazed by God's grace? Are you still available, just as you are, to be used by God?

Passages on fasting and keeping the Sabbath don't exactly set the pulse racing, but underneath them both, we find important truth.

We need to be careful with the 'fasting' passage (vv. 18–22). Some saints, who love their food, have rejoiced that Christ here finally put an end to a rather uncomfortable ritual. But if you read the passage carefully, Jesus is not against fasting at all. In fact in His Sermon on the Mount, He assumes that real disciples will fast – 'When you fast...' (Matt. 6:16). He simply warns against the accompanying showmanship.

And here in Mark, Jesus simply suggested that it was inappropriate for the disciples to fast while He, 'the bridegroom' (what a lovely title, reflecting the loyalty and love of Jesus) was with them (v. 19). Fasting was a sign of godly sorrow, but how could you be sorrowful when Jesus was in your midst? It's interesting that Mark places this fasting passage immediately after Jesus joyfully feasting with sinners!

Fasting is a forgotten jewel of spiritual discipline. In our indulgent culture, it is a way of controlling our bodily appetites, and telling God we feel His Word is more important to us than our daily bread. The early church certainly believed in fasting, and the Holy Spirit spoke to the church at Antioch compellingly, setting apart Paul and Barnabas for mission, during a time of 'worshipping and fasting' (Acts 13:1,2).

Likewise, Jesus would like us to keep some kind of 'Sabbath' in our lives – a special day of the week when we take time to rest, spend time with family and friends, and focus our thoughts on Christ, away from the drivenness of work and consumer culture. However, Sunday can be the least restful day of the week, so perhaps we need to find some other time to give ourselves the body and soul 'rest' that God commands (see Mark 6:31).

So if Jesus is not against fasting, or Sabbath observance, what is He getting at in these passages? Surely it's the truth that religious ritual can actually deaden living faith, depending on how we use it. If you become a slave to fasting, or create 100 rules about what to do and not to do on a Sunday, it is easy to lose the reasons for which these rituals were given, and you end up gauging your 'spirituality' by how often and how zealously you keep the rules.

Once your rule keeping gets to the point where you are indignant over a man being healed – having a deformed arm gloriously restored – simply because it's the Sabbath, then you've lost the purpose of the ritual in the first place. That's what made Jesus angry and 'deeply distressed' (3:5) at the Pharisees.

Whatever (ritual) increases your appreciation of Christ is good; whatever (ritual) dims His light in your life has become an unhealthy distraction, and needs to be reassessed. If you live by that maxim, you will please the Lord more often than not.

REFLECTION

Why not try fasting, and write down in a journal how it affected you? Are you still seeing Christ in your weekly rituals? What is your Sabbath? What do you do on it?

If you have ever battled your way through Christmas shoppers, and slumped back into your sofa at home with feet aching and head bursting, you will know that crowds aren't always a good thing.

Mark seems to suggest that crowds weren't always a good thing for Jesus. He mentions 'a large crowd' (v. 7), 'many people' from a wide geographical location (v. 8), who were 'crowding him'. So much so, in fact, that 'he told his disciples to have a small boat ready for him, *to keep the people from crowding him*' (v. 9).

There was a frenzy with this crowd. They were not coming to Jesus to be taught by Him, but to have their felt needs met – 'those with diseases were pushing forward to touch him' (v. 10). Like a preacher looking out at his congregation on a Sunday, it is difficult to discern true motives in a crowd. What are they really after? What are they looking for?

That's why often in the Gospels Jesus challenges His disciples to come away from the crowds, from the mixed motives, from the group hysteria, to follow Him. It's easy to look like a Christian, singing worship songs in a large crowd on a Sunday. But discipleship is seen less in the Sunday pew and more in the Monday office, or school, or staff room. Who are we when there isn't a crowd to hide behind?

The fascinating aspect of this passage is that the frenzied, confused crowds are contrasted negatively with demons. The evil spirits are crystal clear about who Jesus is. When they 'saw him, they fell down before him and cried out, "You are the Son of God"' (v. 11). The clearest confessions of who Christ is, in this first half of Mark, come from demons!

All of which reminds me of that strange passage in James 2:14–26. James is teaching that our faith must express itself by what we do, how we live. It's not enough to be doctrinally orthodox – it's life transformation that matters to God. The demons know who Jesus is, they declare Him publicly, and they fall on their faces in fear. What makes us so different from demons?

Come away from the crowds and demonstrate your faith in Jesus with a transformed life, not simply with sound doctrine.

REFLECTION

Are you following 'the crowd', or following Christ? Has your doctrine transformed your character?

It's been a busy week in our household, celebrating the birthday of one son, and taxi-ing another around to football, cello lessons and church, while trying to keep the baby fed, watered and content. So I was glad to hear my wife say yesterday, 'We need some time, just the two of us.' It's not that we haven't been in the same room; it's that we haven't spent 'quality' time together, and if you are married with young children, you will know the feeling.

There's a little phrase in this passage about Jesus calling His disciples that we very easily skip over, but we mustn't, because it is the most important part of knowing Jesus. When Jesus calls His disciples to Him, we are told why. And there are two reasons.

The second is the reason we expect: 'that he might send them out to preach and to have authority to drive out demons' (v. 15). Clearly Jesus wanted His disciples to go out and take the message of the kingdom to a lost world. But the first reason He called them was 'that they might be with him' (v. 14). Jesus called His disciples, first and foremost, because He wanted to be with them. And He has called you for exactly the same reason.

A little bit like the 'starry host' in Isaiah 40:26, Jesus names His disciples one by one, 'Simon...John...Andrew, Philip, Bartholomew...' He knows us by name.

He is personally acquainted with all our needs, and He wants to be with us. Some disciples are named here who are never named again in Mark's Gospel. But they are not disciples simply because they do important things for Jesus. They are disciples because He called them to be 'with him'.

You may feel I am labouring the point, but it's probably the most important thing we can learn as believers. I am not simply a pawn to be deployed on God's cosmic chessboard. Before I am His servant, I am His son. And I get the sense in my busy pastoral life that God groans a bit like my wife did yesterday. I am so busy running round doing things for Him that He is longing for me to slow down and rediscover why He called me in the first place – to be 'with him'.

As Martha discovered (Luke 10:38–42), we can exhaust ourselves so much doing good things, we miss out on 'the best', sitting at Jesus' feet. Let this thought go with you today and always: '[He] called...those he wanted...that they might be with him'.

REFLECTION

Are you so busy you have forgotten how to worship? How much 'quality time' do you spend with Jesus each day?

This passage is the one that famously inspired C.S. Lewis to ask if Jesus was mad, bad or God. Jesus' own family (Mary, and presumably His younger brothers, James and Jude and others) think He is mad. His ministry is so hectic He barely has time to eat, and He keeps on casting out demons and claiming victory over Satan. So they come to 'take charge of him' (v. 21).

If Jesus' family think He is mad, the jealous religious leaders claim He is bad, casting out demons with the help of 'the prince of demons' (v. 22). If they had taken a few minutes to think, they would have realized how ridiculous that suggestion was, for it would mean 'a kingdom is divided against itself' (v. 24).

The central theme of these contrasting passages is control. Jesus' family want to control Christ because He is too radical for their liking. The religious leaders want to control Christ because He is too dangerous, threatening to turn their power base upside down.

'Calm down, Jesus. Be more reasonable,' is the message that rings out from family and Pharisee alike. And that is the same message that often rings out from our churches. We do not realize how radical Jesus is, calling for total commitment and taking Satan's territory by storm.

We want a more reasonable Christ who fits in snugly with warm liturgy and senior citizens' tea parties. But Jesus will not be controlled. Rather, He is the one in control, powerful enough to dethrone Satan (v. 27), and radical enough to ask people to leave everything to follow Him (vv. 34,35).

Is your God too small? Have you settled for a pale caricature of Christ you feel comfortable with, and lost sight of the real Jesus who calls you to die to yourself, set aside every competing allegiance, take up your cross and follow Him? A vicar once said, 'Everywhere Paul went, there was a riot or revival; everywhere I go, they serve tea!'

Don't domesticate Jesus. If Jesus is mad or bad, then burn your Bible, leave church and tell your children to have nothing to do with Him. If He is God, give up everything to follow your risen King. But whatever you do, don't reduce Jesus to the category of 'nice'. He hasn't left you that option.

REFLECTION

In what ways could your discipleship be described as 'radical'? Have you submitted your whole life to Jesus' control?

I love a good sandwich – BLTs are my current favourite – where the combination of freshly toasted bread, together with a succulent filling, creates a taste sensation. Mark is also fond of sandwiches, but of a different variety! The outward layer of Mark 4 is the telling (vv. 1–9), and then the explanation (vv. 14–20) of one of Jesus' most famous parables. But the middle part (vv. 10–13), the juicy filling, is where we get the main point of the message.

The message of the parable itself is clear. The word of God, depicted as a 'seed' which needs to be liberally scattered everywhere, always remains the same. Never change the basic content of the message of the gospel, and spread that message as widely as you can, regardless of whether or not people respond.

But that message (of God's grace to save sinners through the death and resurrection of Christ) will be received in different ways, depending on the heart of the listener. Various impediments stop the word from penetrating and changing us. Satan can steal the word away before it even gets in. Sometimes it does get in, but a person is so full of life's worries, or so devoted to personal pleasure, that the word is choked out of them.

For still others, they appear to receive the gospel gladly to begin with, but are not prepared to face the persecution that ensues – they have no root. You may look like you are saved, but the proof of the pudding is perseverance. Only one in four will properly receive the word, and even then, there are differing degrees of how much we make of the word in our lives – some are more fruitful than others.

But that's just the outer layer. The inner message is that our understanding of Jesus' kingdom comes from God revealing it to us. If He does not reveal it to us, we will have no understanding, no matter how clever we are. And God will only reveal the kingdom to those who walk with Jesus – 'The secret of the kingdom of God has been given to you [disciples of Jesus]' (v. 11).

Those who follow Jesus in obedience will be given deeper and deeper insight into the kingdom. Conversely, those who are passengers will always be left on the outside looking in. There are many passengers, even in lively evangelical churches. They look like disciples, but rarely get excited about the kingdom, because it is a closed door to them. In which camp are you?

REFLECTION

Has God's word been fruitful in your life? How do you know?

This little trio of parables builds on the previous Parable of the Sower. The question at the heart of all these parables is, 'Why do so few seem to respond to Jesus?' Such questioning is prompted by the previous chapter where Jesus' own family and religious leaders, who should be the first to respond, seem unable to do so (3:20–35).

It's not that the light is hidden from people (vv. 21–25). The light of the gospel is to shine out everywhere, like a lamp placed on a stand. But you need 'ears to hear' what the gospel really means. To have the right ears is not about having enough intelligence to interpret the Bible, but to have enough hunger to discover Spirit-inspired truth.

That is the meaning behind the strange verse 'Whoever has will be given more; whoever does not have, even what he has will be taken away from him' (v. 25). Jesus isn't talking about money, but about spiritual hunger to know and obey God's will (see 3:34,35). If you have that hunger, God will reveal more and more of His kingdom to you. If you don't have that hunger, the kingdom will remain an unsolved mystery.

But don't think that this kingdom, which seems to be rejected by so many, will remain small forever. The next two parables (vv. 26–34) focus around 'seeds' which grow almost imperceptibly. The kingdom starts small 'like a mustard seed which is the smallest seed you plant', but after a while it 'becomes the largest of all garden plants'. (v. 32)

By the end of Jesus' earthly ministry, the kingdom amounted to the 120 disciples who congregated at the beginning of Acts. Hardly a world-changing movement. But just watch that seed grow! After a while the kingdom tree has 'such big branches that the birds of the air can perch in its shade' (v. 32).

The birds which have flown to the kingdom surely represent the Gentile nations who have since flocked to 'the church'. So the promise of this parable is that God's kingdom will one day rule the world, a promise that prophets such as Isaiah, Daniel and Habakkuk had already made.

Don't be dismayed if your church seems small, or if the number of Christians in your city, town or village appears miniscule. You are part of an invisible, growing kingdom which, when all the power brokers of our world have had their day, will still be standing.

REFLECTION

Are you hungry to obey God's will? Do you share the Bible's unerring confidence that God's kingdom will one day rule the world (see Isa. 2:1–5)?

23

There is an unusual scene in the first *Superman* movie, where an elderly couple suffer a flat tyre, and quite by chance discover a little 'lost' boy by the side of the road (who happens to have arrived inter-galactically from the planet Krypton, but they don't know that yet). The couple are compassionate towards this poor little blue-eyed waif, wondering where his parents have gone. But compassion soon turns to jaw-dropping amazement when the little 5 year old lifts up a one-tonne car single-handedly, allowing the old man to change the flat tyre. The couple stare at each other in disbelief.

Mark 4:35 – 6:6 contains a series of four miracles where Jesus shows His awesome powers over creation, over demons, over sickness, and even over death itself. And Mark places a question on the lips of the crowds who witness them, 'Who then is this?' (see 4:31; 6:2). Through all the stories, Mark focuses on the reaction of the crowds to Jesus – reactions of faith that draw us to Him, or fear that repels us.

Jesus walking on water reveals Him to be nothing less than God incarnate. Because of the bowl shape of Lake Galilee, storms can suddenly flare up out of nowhere, just like the crises that can crash against the shores of our lives. And just as in our own traumas, God often seems asleep, and we need to 'wake him' through prayer, and ask Him if He cares about our traumas.

What the disciples needed to learn, and what we need to learn, is that no storm is bigger than the God who journeys with us. It is a sign of how much we really know Christ if we ask ourselves, 'Are we more afraid of Him, or of the crises?' The moral of this story is not that Jesus will automatically calm every storm in our life. We know from experience that isn't true, and the Bible teaches us that sometimes lengthy storms are necessary to refine our characters (Rom. 8:28).

The point is that Jesus is more glorious than any crisis we may face. And faith means trusting in His sovereign power, even when He doesn't calm the storm. Again Mark invites us to ask, 'Is your vision of Jesus even close to how glorious He truly is?' and what difference does that make to your trust in Him?

REFLECTION

Do you need to trust God more? How do you react when Jesus doesn't calm the storms in your life?

READ Mark 5:1–20

What image do you have in your mind of the devil? Horns? Angel of light? The sheer number of exorcisms in Mark confronts us with the personality of the Evil One. Satan's origins are mysterious, but we must not relegate him to the humorous cartoon figure clutching a pitchfork. He's much too involved in our families, our community and our church to dismiss.

Intriguingly, Mark suggests that the storm Jesus calmed on the way to Gerasene territory was stirred up by demons. The same word is used for Jesus 'rebuking' the storm as 'rebuking' the demons. Satan reigns in Gerasene territory and he doesn't want the kingdom of God to break in. And if we truly grasped the heavenly conflict that sets the backdrop for our everyday lives, we would spend much more time on our knees praying for our marriages, our children, our church, and our neighbours, who are held under Satan's sway (Eph. 2:1–3).

Amazingly, the Gerasenes seem more comfortable with Satan than Jesus. They are used to the wild man cutting himself, naked in the caves. (Satan wants to destroy the image of God in humanity.) But when Jesus releases the man from satanic oppression, and they find him 'dressed and in his right mind' (v. 15), they implore Christ to leave!

Jesus unsettles them and they haul up a massive 'do not disturb' sign over their souls. Are you willing for Jesus to unsettle you, and call you to radical kingdom living, or have you snuggled into a Satan-owned world of pleasure, comfort and selfish interest which you do not want disrupted?

The healed demoniac is a model disciple who has so experienced Christ's love and power that he wants to follow Him wherever He goes – 'he begged to go with him' (v. 18). Discipleship means simply going wherever Jesus goes. Often, of course, the hardest place to go is not 'darkest Africa' on mission, but to stay at home with family and neighbours, and your frustrating local church, and be a missionary there for Christ, telling them how much Jesus has done for you (v. 20).

That's what Jesus tells a healed demoniac to do, and He may well be telling you to get stuck in right where you are.

REFLECTION

Do you have a 'do not disturb' sign written over your life? Where is God calling you to serve Him?

The former Liverpool football manager Bill Shankly once famously said, 'Some people believe football is a matter of life and death. I am very disappointed with that attitude. I can assure you it is much, much more important than that.' But this passage from Mark reminds us that nothing is more important than life and death.

In yet another story-within-a-story, we find two very different people – Jairus, a named and respected 'synagogue ruler' (vv. 21–24; vv. 35–43), and an unnamed woman who wants to melt away in the crowds (vv. 25–34). Yet both the famed synagogue ruler and this obscure, nervous lady come to Jesus in desperate need. Crises like death and illness are the great levellers in life, and often it takes a crisis before we will cry out to Jesus.

What Jesus requires from both is faith. The nervous lady, who had been subject to bleeding for twelve years and could find no doctor to help, came and touched Jesus (v. 27). Her touch was clearly different from that of the crowds milling around. Jesus picks her out from the pressing crowds, and declares, 'Daughter, your *faith* has healed you' (v. 34).

Meanwhile, Jairus receives the kind of news every father dreads: 'Your daughter is dead…Why bother the teacher any more?' (v. 35.) Jesus seems almost insensitive – dismissive of the power of death: 'Don't be afraid; just believe' (v. 36). Faith makes the difference between life and death, faith in a Christ who can calm storms, heal demoniacs, do what no doctor can do, and who is Lord even over death itself.

What a beautiful eyewitness (probably Peter) touch, when Mark preserves the very words in Aramaic that Jesus uttered to breathe life into a dead girl's body: '*Talitha koum!*' (Little girl, get up.) Note that Jesus has already dismissed the unbelieving crowds (v. 40). Unbelievers aren't allowed to see displays of Christ's glory like this. It is faith that unlocks the power of Jesus.

Listen to Jesus whisper to your heart today, 'Don't be afraid; just believe.' There is no crisis in life where Jesus is not Lord. And even when we reach that final shoreline marked 'death' – the one that fills us with Jairus-esque dread, even then, *especially* then, the risen Lord Jesus Christ beckons to us with divine power, 'Don't be afraid; just believe.' Even death, that great impostor to God's creation plan, has 'lost its sting.' (see 1 Cor. 15:55–57) 'Don't be afraid; just believe.'

REFLECTION

Does it take a crisis before you will call out to Jesus? Do you believe He has power over death?

I'll never forget queuing up at passport control the first time I visited America. The most sullen man imaginable, with a holstered revolver hanging from his waist, asked me why I was coming to the USA. He seemed resentful that my papers were valid, and half grunted as he ushered me through. I have since had many wonderful weeks in the States, but my first few moments made me feel I was distinctly unwelcome.

Mark 6 is a chilling reminder that Christ and His followers are unwelcome in this world. Jesus comes back to His 'hometown' (vv. 1–6) having calmed storms, exorcized demons, and raised the dead. He even preaches with stirring wisdom (v. 2). But the people can't see past His humble 'carpenter' status, refuse to countenance that He is a prophet, but instead 'took offence at him' (v. 3).

Then, as Jesus sends His disciples out on preaching tours (vv. 7–13), He gets them to travel light (they won't be staying long anywhere they go), 'And if any place will not welcome you or listen to you, shake the dust off your feet when you leave, as a testimony against them' (v. 11). The gospel we preach will get a frosty reception from the majority of people with whom we try to share it. We need to live as pilgrims, with our backpacks, knowing that 'this world is not our home'.

And to hammer home the point, the passage ends with the beheading of John the Baptist (vv. 14–29). His crime was to confront Herod's immorality – it's what a prophet is meant to do. But Herodias will have none of it, forcing Herod into a corner while her daughter dances a sensual dance, and requesting the head of the Baptist on a platter. What a graphic depiction of what Paul later warned Timothy – 'those who live godly lives will be persecuted' (see 2 Tim. 3:12).

If you are feeling unwelcome because of your Christian commitment at work, or even in your family home, then do not be surprised. This is the burden we need to carry as followers of the Man of Sorrows who 'came to…his own, but his own did not receive him' (John 1:11). Don't let that stop you living a provocative Christian life – it's what a prophet's meant to do.

But always remember, you're not really 'home' yet. John's disciples coming and honouring him in burial (v. 29) is a subtle pointer to the glory and honour that awaits those whose holiness is out of step with a hostile world.

REFLECTION

Does your lifestyle make you feel 'unwelcome' in this world? How often do you think about heaven, glory and rewards?

As I write, Europe is facing an economic crisis, Libya has followed Egypt in dethroning its dictator, London was recently the scene of street riots, and Aberdeen's figures for drug abuse have reached a record high. It is a troubled world we live in. But there is an answer!

The answer is not political or economic – it's Christ. In this famous passage, Jesus offers Himself as

1. Rest for the weary. Jesus tells His disciples, exhausted by intense ministry and the constant pressure of crowds, to 'Come with me by yourselves to a quiet place and get some rest' (v. 31). Jesus offers us rest – not just physical rest (though that is so important for busy, driven Christians), but spiritual rest. He invites His disciples on a retreat with Him. How much time are you spending simply in Jesus' uncluttered presence, allowing Him to give you spiritual and emotional 'rest'? He invites you to 'come'.

2. Direction for the lost. Jesus' retreat plan was thwarted by the crowds who chased Him round the lake's edge. They were 'like sheep without a shepherd' (v. 34), lacking any kind of direction in life, so 'he began teaching them many things' (v. 34). You need Christ's teaching to guide your life, dictate your decisions, and set boundaries for your behaviour. How much is Christ's word dwelling in you richly (see Col. 3:16)?

3. Satisfaction for the soul. It was getting late, and the people hadn't eaten, leading to this glorious, Christ-fuelled feast. Christ was telling the people He was the same God who fed their forefathers on manna in the desert for forty years. But instead of manna, Christ offers us Himself – the Living Bread – so that we can feast on Him eternally. 'If you eat of me, you will live forever' (see John 6:51). Don't give in to the lie that the world's pleasures can truly satisfy you. They are transitory and leave you empty. But as the psalmist said, 'God is the strength of my heart and my portion forever' (Ps. 73:26). Feast on Jesus, through Scripture, prayer, fellowship with other believers, praise and thanksgiving, and there will be enough to fuel your soul for time and for eternity!

REFLECTION

Do you truly believe that Christ offers ultimate satisfaction? Are you feasting on His Word, and practising His presence, every day?

'Man looks at the outward appearance, but the LORD looks at the heart' (1 Sam. 16:7). That was the truth that shone out when the shepherd boy, David, the youngest brother in the family, the one who Jesse did not bother presenting before the prophet Samuel, was anointed king of Israel, rather than his more burly, outwardly impressive older brothers.

We need to keep that truth burning in our hearts, especially when our lives are full of the kind of ritual that can easily descend into legalism. Do we assess our spirituality according to how well we keep the rules, relying on outward appearance rather than heart transformation? In this passage, Jesus defends true 'heart' religion against the backdrop of 'the tradition of the elders' (v. 3), a morose cocktail of unbiblical rules and regulations thought up by scribes over the centuries, ironically to make sure Jews kept the law.

But 'the tradition of the elders' had risen to enjoy equal status with the Word of God, and the average Jew felt that faithful Judaism meant obeying the traditions, rather than searching your heart to see if you were truly loving God. For example, if a Jew went to the marketplace, where he would come into contact with Gentiles, he had to have a ritual bath when he came home, to make himself clean (v. 4)! If you have 100 similar rules to follow – and Mark adds 'they observe many other traditions' (v. 4) – then your life can simply become making sure you look right on the outside; who cares what is going on in your heart?

That's why Jesus moves from His debate with the Pharisees (vv. 1–13) to talk to the crowds (note the transition in v. 14). This was not just a technical legal debate about the place tradition should have. Jesus was highlighting a tendency in all human religion to rely on show rather than reality. 'Nothing outside a man can make him "unclean"... Rather, it is what comes out of a man that makes him "unclean"' (v. 15).

'Test your hearts,' says Jesus. It's from the human heart that 'evil thoughts, sexual immorality, theft, murder, adultery, greed, malice, deceit' and so on emanate. (vv. 21,22) No outward act – not baptism, not communion, not tithing your income, not even deeds of mercy – can cover up what is going on in our hearts.

Socrates once said, 'The unexamined life is not worth living.' Or, as the psalmist put it, 'Search me, O God, and know my heart' (Ps. 139:23).

REFLECTION

How often do you examine your heart? Are there 'traditions' in your life or church that keep you from Jesus?

Even if you have never seen the iconic science fiction series *Star Trek*, you probably know the phrase that made it famous – 'to boldly go where no man has gone before'. That is what Jesus is doing in this passage as He enters Gentile territory; firstly 'Tyre' (vv. 24–30), then 'Sidon' (vv. 31–37).

When you realize that every morning some Jewish males used to pray, 'Lord, I thank you that I am not a Gentile, a slave or a woman', you begin to understand what a bold move this was. But Christ is a boundary breaker.

The point is underlined when Jesus interacts with a Gentile woman – women were a sub-class in Jewish society – who had a demon-possessed child (demon possession was the ultimate in 'uncleanness'). What boundaries are we prepared to cross to bring the gospel to lost people – racial, social, economic? With the church in the West losing numbers at a rapid rate, we must go where people are, rather than waiting for them to be 'acceptable' to us at Sunday morning church.

If Jesus is the boundary breaker, He is also the faith provoker. He does not make it easy for this Gentile lady, and even appears rude: 'it is not right to take the children's bread and toss it to their dogs' (v. 27). The 'children' are the Jews, and the 'dogs' are Gentiles – not very nice! What is Jesus playing at?

But Jesus knows this lady's heart, and is waiting to see if His provocative words will draw faith from her. And she gives a brilliant reply which shows she is hungry for Christ's grace – 'even the dogs under the table eat the children's crumbs' (v. 28). Christ cannot resist the woman's faith, and assures her that her daughter is healed.

The final scene reveals Jesus not simply as the boundary breaker, or the faith provoker, but also the 'great Creator'. This time He is in the neighbouring town of Sidon (v. 31), where He meets a deaf man who 'could hardly talk' (v. 32). If Christ can conquer social and religious boundaries, He can also conquer physical ones – deaf and mute together suggest unusually difficult physical limitations.

Christ, of course, could heal without any melodrama, but He deliberately touches the man's tongue with His spit, reminiscent of God breathing life into Adam's nostrils, and speaks the word that reopens the man's ears – with an accompanying 'sigh', reflecting His frustration at a sin-marred creation. And suddenly we are back in Genesis 1, watching the great Creator at work!

Why does Mark include the story of the feeding of the 4,000 (vv. 1–10), when he has already told us about the feeding of the 5,000? As you read the story, you realize it is almost a carbon copy, bar a few minor differences. But perhaps that's the point!

While the feeding of the 5,000 has a clearly Jewish setting, and the twelve baskets left over represent the twelve tribes of Israel, the 4,000 is set in a Gentile context. Jesus has just completed a ministry tour of Tyre and Sidon, and it is 'During those days' (v. 1), in Gentile territory, that He feeds the 4,000. Seven basketfuls are left over this time, a number that represents fullness in Scripture. The point of the story is that Jesus is just as sufficient a Saviour for the Gentile as for the Jew – for the 'outcast' as well as the 'insider'.

How ironic that following one of Jesus' major miraculous signs, He is questioned 'back home' by the Pharisees for His failure to produce 'a sign from heaven' (vv. 11–13)! Mark tells us Jesus 'sighed deeply' (v. 12). He had previously sighed when He came across a deaf and mute man in Gentile territory. Now He sighs before the spiritual deafness of Pharisees, who were the self-proclaimed guardians of pure Judaism, but could not recognize the Son of God when He walked into their neighbourhood (see John 1:12).

'Jews demand miraculous signs', said Paul later, 'and Greeks look for wisdom, but we preach Christ crucified' (1 Cor.

1:22,23). Christ will never satisfy the miracle chasers, or the sophisticates. His cross stands against all forms of human pride and celebrity. It is the naked Christ, gasping for air, utterly broken, who is our redemption, but He will always be out of reach for those who want the spectacular.

But it's not just Pharisaic deafness that frustrates Christ; it's the blindness of His own disciples (vv. 14–21). They are worried about having no bread, when they have just witnessed the King of glory multiplying loaves for thousands! He can barely hide His exasperation: 'Do you have eyes but fail to see, and ears but fail to hear?' (v. 18).

Before we are too hard on the Twelve, could it be that we, too, His modern-day disciples, begin to doubt Him, not long after He has shown His amazing faithfulness in some way in our lives? Does Jesus sigh when He thinks about your faith and mine? After He has revealed Himself to us, and proved Himself time and again, 'Do [we] still not understand?' (v. 21).

REFLECTION

Why did God choose to save us through a cross rather than something more spectacular? Is there anything about your faith that Jesus might find frustrating? Praise God He is God of Gentiles, as well as Jews.

Peter's confession of Jesus as 'Christ' or Messiah is the exact centre point of Mark's Gospel, and from here on the whole tone and message of the gospel will change. Up to now, Jesus has been zigzagging across Lake Galilee in a whirlwind ministry. From this point on He will 'set his face' (Luke 9:51, NKJV) to journey south to Jerusalem, the 'lion's den'. Up to this point He has been casting out demons and performing miracles left, right and centre. From now on there is barely an exorcism, but much more teaching for His disciples as He prepares them for the cross.

So this passage is the turning point of the whole gospel. And Mark includes the story of the healing of a blind man, as a precursor to Peter's confession of Jesus. This healing story is the only 'two stage' miracle in all the Gospels. When Jesus first puts His hands on the man's eyes, he replies, 'I see people; they look like trees walking around' (v. 24). Although some vision had been restored, the recovery of full sight awaits a second touch from Christ (v. 25).

The same is true for Peter and the disciples. Peter receives a glorious but partial revelation of who Jesus is: 'You are the Christ' (v. 29). The first half of the Gospel has been leading up to this revelation. Jesus is the long-awaited Messiah, the anointed one of God, sent to release God's people from their enemies and usher in a kingdom of righteousness, justice and peace.

But Peter's sight is blurred. He needs a second touch from Jesus. When Jesus tells His bewildered followers that 'the Son of Man must suffer many things and be rejected...' (v. 31), Peter takes Jesus aside to rebuke Him. That wasn't a script any Jew could stomach. Wasn't the Messiah meant to be a conquering King? That's how every Jew read the messianic prophecies.

But Jesus had to re-educate them, in line with the 'Suffering Servant' passages of Isaiah. Before the Messiah will reign as King, He must go to a cross in shame and humiliation, to deal with the sin that was a much greater threat to God's people than any foreign invader.

If that was hard to take for blurry-eyed disciples, even harder was the truth that anyone who wanted to follow Jesus must 'deny himself and take up his cross and follow me' (v. 34). Suffering was the pathway to glory for Jesus, and for any disciple who wants to follow in His footsteps!

Do you need Jesus to open your eyes again, in a deeper way, to understand the path of suffering He is calling you to as His disciple?

REFLECTION

Praise God today for the suffering Christ endured to save us. To what extent are you carrying your cross today?

What does it mean to say we know Jesus? Which Jesus? Kevin de Young, an American pastor, says that Jesus is one of the most popular people in America. But there are so many 'Jesuses' out there. There's 'Open-minded Jesus' who loves everyone all the time, no matter what. There's 'Martyr Jesus', a good man who died a cruel death so we can feel sorry for Him. There's 'Good Example Jesus', who shows you how to help people, change the planet, and become a better you. There's 'Boyfriend Jesus' who wraps His arms around us as we sing of His intoxicating love. But Mark's vision of Jesus in this great Transfiguration passage dispels the pale caricatures and shows us the real Christ, and what it takes to know Him. Mark calls us to

• **Revere the Person of Jesus.** For a brief moment on top of the mountain, the place of divine revelation in Scripture, the veil drops, and the three disciples get a taste of Christ's pre-incarnate glory – 'His clothes became dazzling white' (v. 3). Jesus is the same God Isaiah saw in his Temple vision, where angels cover their faces and feet and cry 'Holy, holy, holy.' He is not our pal. He loves us and sympathizes with us, but He is also the eternal God whom we should worship with reverence and fear.

• **Accept the Uniqueness of Jesus.** Moses, representing the Law, and Elijah, the Prophets, appear with Jesus (v. 4) – a subtle way of telling us that the whole Old Testament is pointing to, and finds its fulfilment in, the person of Christ. What He will do through His death and resurrection in Jerusalem will reverse the curse of Adam's fall, fulfil promises to Abraham to bless the nations of the earth, and open the way for fallen humanity to dwell in the New Jerusalem. Christianity is Christ. There is no other way to God but through this glorious Lord Jesus, fully God and fully man, the unique answer to humanity's deepest need. Paul will later sum up the whole Christian message with the phrase, 'the Gospel of God['s] ... Son' (Rom. 1:1,3).

• **Follow the Pathway of Jesus.** The disciples come down the mountain in every way (v. 9). Christ reminds them (again) that He is going to suffer, just like the new Elijah, John the Baptist, suffered at Herod's hands (vv. 11–13). Jesus won't contemplate glory without suffering, and following Jesus means we must suffer as His followers before we too enter our glory.

REFLECTION

Has Jesus' glory dimmed in your heart in any way? Are you prepared to share in His suffering before you share in His glory?

I was speaking to a lady recently who told me how tough her life had become after her baptism. Following the euphoria of the event, she said that she had never experienced so many spiritual attacks in such a short space of time.

From the mountaintop to the valley – that is the experience for so many of us. And it was the experience Jesus went through as He came down the Mount of Transfiguration to a scene of chaos. His disciples could not cast out a demon, and a tormented father with frail faith was crying out for help! Is there not a challenge here that the church cannot remain aloof, contemplating the attributes of Christ on a mountaintop, when a lost and struggling world needs Christ's redeeming power?

The vulnerable father's interaction with Christ is so touching. He had lived with a demon-possessed boy for years, worn down, no doubt, trying to protect his son from the demon's destructive power (v. 22). The father approaches Christ with what little faith he has – 'if you can do anything, take pity on us and help us' (v. 22). Jesus tries to draw more faith from him: 'Everything is possible for him who believes' (v. 23). But does the father have enough faith? An answer of 'I do believe; help me overcome my unbelief!' is disarmingly honest, but hardly reassuring (v. 24).

Yet Jesus does for this man what He has done for those in Mark who are full of faith – 'I command you, come out of him, and never enter him again' (v. 25). Christ's miracle is emphatic and complete, and seems to be much greater than the amount of faith placed in Him!

But I think that's the point. It is not the size of our faith, but the power of our Saviour that matters. You may feel just as fragile as this broken father, bewildered by life scenarios that are as horrendous as his. You want to have faith in a mighty God, but life has almost crushed it out of you.

If that is where you are today, surely this story is an encouragement – come to Christ with whatever scraps of faith you have, even if it's no more than saying, 'Help me, Lord', and watch what Jesus will do! The thief on the cross simply said to Jesus, in his dying breath, 'remember me' (Luke 23:42). Hardly a deep prayer of repentance. Yet our powerful Saviour took that scrap of faith from a wreck of a man, and promised him Paradise.

REFLECTION

What difficult situation do you need to entrust to Jesus today? Remember, it's not the amount of faith you have, but who your faith is in that counts. As Robert Murray McCheyne said, 'For every one look at self, take ten looks at Christ.'

'Take up your cross and follow me' is almost a theme sentence for the second half of Mark's Gospel. Jesus tells His disciples three times in chapters 8, 9 and 10 that He is heading to the cross. He is not simply warning His disciples so that they will be emotionally ready for when it happens: He is preparing them for true discipleship.

At first glance these disparate passages seem like a ragbag of disconnected themes. But Jesus' passion prediction (vv. 31,32) acts as a heading for this section. How ought we to live in light of a Saviour who has humbled Himself all the way to a cross?

Firstly, we need to get rid of all pride (vv. 33–37). As Jesus is telling His disciples that He is on His way to a cross, the disciples are arguing with each other about who among them is the greatest! The irony is tragic. So Jesus teaches them, 'anyone who wants to be first…must be…the servant of all' (v. 35). Christ will be first in the coming kingdom, given a name that is above every name, precisely because He came to serve us on a cross. The way up in the kingdom is the way down.

Secondly, we are called to accept the humble, the poor and the outcast. Jesus places a little child in front of His disciples and says, 'Whoever welcomes one of these little children…welcomes me' (v. 37). The church ought to be made up of an unusual number of the poor and vulnerable, and we need to make time for the orphan and the widow. True disciples should also accept other miracle workers (vv. 38–41) who are not in their band, 'for whoever is not against us is for us.' (v. 40) Evangelicals should not become a private clique that believes that God cannot be at work outside their elite group. That is arrogant and unworthy of the cross.

Thirdly, suffering is a necessary ingredient of discipleship. Better to suffer the loss of a hand, a foot or an eye, than be led into sin. Jesus is using hyperbole here to show us that growing in righteousness is a painful business, demanding us to crucify whatever passions or desires run contrary to God's kingdom.

All of these passages ultimately point to the same truth – 'If anyone will come after me, he must deny himself and take up his cross and follow me' (8:34). We follow a rugged Messiah who turns the values of our self-seeking culture upside down.

REFLECTION

To what extent has Christ turned your values upside down? In what way will you 'deny yourself' today?

Discipleship is so practical. It affects our marriages (vv. 1–12), how we bring up our children (vv. 13–16), and how we handle possessions (vv. 17–31). You don't show yourself a true disciple by shaving your head, taking a vow of silence, and retreating to a monastery. You show it in the day-to-day realities of family life and bank accounts.

The permanence of marriage, even in conservative Jewish circles in Jesus' day, was not respected. The Hillel school of rabbis taught that a man could divorce his wife if she did not please him in some way. Times have not really changed; as the divorce rate in Europe soars, one couple asked recently if they could change their marriage vows to 'for as long as we both shall love'.

So Jesus reminds His questioners that God intended marriage to be a lifelong commitment, where a husband and wife serve and protect each other. A man 'leaves' his father and mother and 'cleaves' to his wife (v. 7). Sex is not for one-night stands. It is a deep personal union between soul mates – reserved exclusively for the marriage bond. It is the one time in life when a man and a woman are able to return to the naked innocence of Eden, and such a gift should not be taken lightly.

God is calling us here to fight for our marriages – to work hard at protecting this sacred covenant bond. Don't let a thirst for happiness destroy your call to holiness! The Matthew 19 parallel passage does suggest that couples are permitted divorce if a spouse has been sexually unfaithful, but we should not be looking for the 'get out' clause in marriage, as much as seeking to replicate God's original creation intent.

That a passage on the ugliness of divorce should be followed by the warning not to hinder children from entering the kingdom (vv. 13–16) only serves to highlight how deeply the quality or otherwise of our marriages affects the development – social and spiritual – of our children. As a wise pastor once said, 'If you want to show your children how much you love them, love their mother.'

REFLECTION

Are you pursuing discipleship in your marriage? Do your children see that Christ is your highest priority?

A rich man came to Jesus with impressive zeal. He addressed Christ with honour – 'Good teacher' – and his question was not the kind of trick question other religious leaders tended to throw at Jesus. This man genuinely wanted to know 'what must I do to inherit eternal life?' (v. 17). If sincerity was enough to win a place in the kingdom, this man was first on the list. But his problem was in the verb 'do'.

We all want to do something to be good enough for God. But Jesus demolishes all such pretensions with a single phrase – 'No one is good – except God alone' (v. 18). Nothing we 'do' can make us righteous before God. The gospel is a message of grace, not a merit system. It is about what God has done for us in Christ, not about how many commandments we have kept. As Vance Havner put it, 'all other religions say "do, do, do". Christianity says "done"!'

Saving faith, in this man's context, involved not so much keeping a tick list of commands, but giving up the thing he held most precious, so that he could fully commit to Christ, the Saviour. Sadly, the thing that this zealous, upstanding, sincere man found most precious was his money.

The people of India often have trouble with monkeys. And so they set very clever traps for them. They put a banana in a jar that is attached to the ground. The jar is just wide enough for the monkey to get his hand in. But while the monkey is grasping hold of the banana, he can't get his hand out of the jar. If he lets go of the banana, he can free himself. But monkeys love their bananas so much, that even when they see their trapper coming, they won't let go. They *can't* let go. They want the banana too much.

We can all be a bit like those monkeys when it comes to our love of money. However much this rich young ruler desired eternal life, and respected Christ, he loved money just a little bit more. He could not let go of the security his money gave him to find eternal security in Christ. How tragic! But are we so different? Jesus spoke more about the danger of money than He did about prayer. Our attitude to money can keep us from heaven. It can also prevent us from amounting to much in the kingdom.

Cross-carrying discipleship means denying yourself, holding on loosely to possessions. To carry the cross, we need to loosen our grip on our wallets. Or as Jesus put it, 'where your treasure is, there your heart will be also' (Matt. 6:21).

REFLECTION

What does your credit card statement say about your commitment to Christ? Are you tithing?

There is a subtle pathos in this passage, as Mark tells us Jesus was 'leading the way' to Jerusalem. We know why He is going – for the third and final time He predicts His suffering and death. He is leading the way as our Saviour, to hang on a cross as God's appointed sacrifice for sin.

The question is, 'Who will follow him on His path of suffering?' And we have an ironic contrast between the disciples, who are busy trying to get the best seat in the house in God's future kingdom (vv. 35–45), and blind Bartimaeus (vv. 46–52).

At the end of the Bartimaeus healing story, Mark says 'he received his sight and *followed Jesus along the road*' (v.52). The disciples are not, in that deeper sense, following Jesus along the road that will lead to suffering and shame. They're too busy talking about glory: 'Let one of us sit at your right and the other at your left in your glory' (v. 37).

Jesus tells His disciples that, in one sense, they cannot follow Him where He is going. 'Can you drink the cup I drink or be baptised with the baptism I am baptised with?' (v. 38) The 'cup' is used several times in the Old Testament to speak about God's wrath. Jesus must be plunged into, He must be 'baptised' into, the wrath of His Father to deal with our sin. That is a place where only He can go, as the spotless Lamb of God.

But there is another sense in which the disciples can, and indeed must, follow Him. That's why Jesus says, strangely, 'You will drink the cup I drink'. Following Jesus will inevitably bring suffering in its wake. As we follow in this fallen world, we must be ready to bear the shame and reproach He bore as our Man of Sorrows.

Are you willing to do that? To stand out from the crowd and nail your colours to the mast as a Christ-follower? Are you ready to give until it hurts, and face rejection from, perhaps, friends and family? Jesus has no time for sleepy followers who play it safe and retreat into the shadows, dreaming of an easy path to glory. Has the time come for you to 'follow Him on the road'?

If you are facing strain in your life right now for following Christ, don't count that unusual. Jesus told us it would be this way. He said 'take up your cross and follow me', and you are honouring Him in the struggle you are facing. Suffering is the pathway to glory.

REFLECTION

Thank Jesus today for taking the wrath of God against your sin, at the cross. Ask Him for strength to live a life worthy of His suffering.

And so Jesus arrives in Jerusalem, for Passion Week, in the last great section (chs. 11–16), of this action-packed Gospel. Mark's emphasis, as Jesus enters the 'lion's den' where He will lay down His life for the sins of the world, is to magnify the worth of Christ. A crucified Messiah was unthinkable for a Jew. That Jesus would end up hanging from a cross as a criminal – a place of ignomiy and shame – created a huge stumbling block for first-century people accepting the gospel.

So Mark wants to remind us, before Jesus arrives at Golgotha, that the man who will hang in shame on that centre cross is a person of inestimable worth. A.W. Tozer said, 'The heaviest obligation lying upon the Christian church today is to purify and elevate her concept of Christ until it is once more worthy of him.'[1]

Jesus, riding into Jerusalem on a donkey, is intentionally fulfilling Zechariah's messianic prophecy, 'Rejoice greatly... Daughter of Jerusalem! See, your king comes to you' (Zech. 9:9). Jesus is deliberately proclaiming Himself the Messiah-King, the fulfilment of all those Old Testament prophecies that point to God's chosen servant who would sit on David's throne, usher in a worldwide kingdom of peace and righteousness, and judge the nations. He is a humble king, gently riding a donkey – a king who is about to lay down His life – but His humility should not hide His universal kingship.

Mark also emphasizes Jesus' sovereignty. He is able to supernaturally direct His disciples to find the unbroken colt on which the King will ride into Jerusalem (vv. 2–6). When the disciples are questioned about taking the colt, they say, 'The Lord needs it'. Normally the disciples call Jesus 'Master', but here they unusually call Him 'Lord', the same title as God.

Jesus is the Sovereign Lord, and the Messiah-King. To borrow Luke's version of the triumphal entry, 'if we don't worship him, the very rocks will cry out in worship.'

But notice the anti-climax in this passage. After all the palm-branch waving and cloak-spreading for the messianic King, we're told that when Jesus finally got to the Temple in Jerusalem 'it was already late' (v. 11). The triumphal entry is followed by a quiet retreat back home – all the crowds have dispersed now.

Is Mark telling us something about the danger of hysteria? These same crowds who cheered, within a week will be shouting 'Crucify Him!' Do we still follow Jesus when the music fades, the big event is over, and life is either dull or full of frustrations?

REFLECTION

Are you purifying and elevating your concept of Jesus? Do you follow Him when the excitement has died down?

A picture paints a thousand words. Mark gives us a picture (v. 11) of the Jewish Messiah 'look[ing] around at everything' in the Jewish Temple. He uses a strong verb meaning literally 'to scrutinise' or 'stare intently at'. The verse is an introduction to the next three chapters (11–13), all situated around the Temple precincts, where the Lord of the Temple will scan His eye over corrupt Jewish religion.

It all begins with the strange account of Jesus cursing the fig tree (vv. 12–14). This story has troubled many people, including the atheist Bertrand Russell who felt it was a sign of unworthy anger. But the fig tree episode, where Jesus withers the tree for its unfruitfulness, is a picture of Jesus' judgement of Jerusalem's unfruitful Temple, and the false worship that pervaded Jewish society.

Mark tells the story in his typical sandwich format – verses 12 to 14 and 20 to 21 tell about the fig tree, and the meat in the sandwich (vv. 15–19) sees Jesus turning over the tables of the sellers who were degrading the holy Temple by turning it into a market stall for merchandise. Is Mark telling us that we seek money more than we seek God, and make it our idol? The tallest building in the London skyline 100 years ago was St Paul's Cathedral. Today the cathedral is dwarfed by the giant towers of Canary Wharf in London's financial district. Does that not show us where we place our priorities? Our finances matter more to us than God does.

Jesus calls us away from false idols to seek the Father with all our hearts, most fervently expressed in faithful prayer (vv. 22–25). Jesus emphasizes believing prayer. He is not suggesting the 'name it and claim it' theology of prosperity teachers, but seriously challenging us that asking God for things we don't think He can do is idolatrous. God is able to do 'more than all we ask or imagine' (Eph. 3:20), and if we limit His supremacy we can't expect Him to answer our prayers.

Finally (vv. 27–33), the question of Jesus' authority comes up again, no doubt because of His bold, public act of condemning Temple worship. This itinerant Galilean preacher has more authority than all the scribes put together. He casts out demons, raises the dead, walks on water, welcomes Gentiles, reinterprets the Sabbath, castigates corrupt Judaism, and binds Satan. We either bow to His authority or are crushed by it. This is the Lord Jesus Christ.

REFLECTION

Is your life producing fruit? Do you believe God can do 'more than all you ask or imagine'?

Jesus certainly wasn't scared of confrontation! A parable like this was bound to sign His death warrant – they 'looked for a way to arrest him' (v. 12) after hearing it – but, like John the Baptist before Him, Christ was not going to hold back from declaring the truth, even if it cost Him. I wonder, do we hold back when some awkward moral issue comes up at work, or in discussion with a neighbour?

It is poignant that the central image of this parable is a vineyard. Vines and vineyards were repeated images for Israel in the Old Testament, and Isaiah 5 represents God's condemnation of His people for failing to be a fruitful vine. The God who had given Israel His law, a temple to worship in, and who had made Israel a numerous nation, expected some yield from His investment. Likewise, the God who has given us His Son, His Holy Spirit, and a worldwide, international church, expects some fruit from His kingdom.

God sent prophets to Israel to gather in the fruit, but they were mistreated. What a thankless task it was for everyone from Elijah, who faced up to Ahab and Jezebel, to Isaiah, who was sawn in two, to Jeremiah, the weeping prophet. The criticism that Paul and his ministry colleagues often faced when bringing God's word to wayward New Testament churches reminds us that God's spokesmen must still be prepared to suffer in order to fulfil their calling.

'But surely they will listen to my son,' thought the landowner. Surely, even if they felt a certain antagonism against him, they would be too fearful to abuse the owner's own flesh and blood. The parable highlights what a dreadful thing it would be for Israel to put God's own Son to death. While God would accomplish redemption through His Son's pain, those leaders whose jealousy and treachery led to His death should tremble with fear. 'What… will the owner of the vineyard do [to the tenants]?'

It reminds us just how personally God takes our response to the gospel. The gospel is not a set of propositions to believe, but a glorious person to be embraced. All of God's passions are stirred by His Son, and how we treat Him. It is God's will that 'The stone the builders rejected' should become the 'cornerstone' (1 Pet. 2:6,7). All of God's plans for the future of our world revolve around Christ, the 'cornerstone'. The success or failure of our lives boils down to how precious or otherwise He becomes to us.

REFLECTION

How precious is God's Son to you? Are you prepared to be persecuted to stand up for Him?

As the tension between Jesus and the religious leaders escalates, Christ is confronted with three questions in this passage from different groups within the Sanhedrin. The Jewish ruling council was made up of Pharisees, Sadducees and scribes. The Pharisees ask Jesus about taxes (vv. 13–17), the Sadducees about marriage and the afterlife (vv. 18–27), and the scribes about the greatest commandment (vv. 28–34).

At the end of these questions, Mark comments 'no one dared asked him any more questions' (v. 34), the implication being that Christ had thoroughly mastered His opponents. And so the final question comes from Him (vv. 35–40), and is not based around peripheral issues such as taxes or marriage, but around His own person, 'How is it that the teachers of the law say that the Christ is the son of David?' (v. 35).

Often the questions people bring to God are smokescreen questions. The Sanhedrin weren't asking about taxes and marriage because they wanted to hear the word of the Lord – they were trying to trap Christ. And often you find this with sceptics. They come out with stretching questions: 'What about evil in the world? How can there be a hell? Can we believe in miracles? How does the Bible square with Darwinian evolution?'

These are important questions, but they can often be a smokescreen, avoiding the ultimate question, 'Who is Jesus?' When Christ takes centre stage that is where He directs the conversation. And He hones in on Psalm 110, the most quoted psalm in the New Testament. Hebrews devotes a large chunk of its exposition to explaining this psalm.

David is the composer of Psalm 110, and describes God talking to someone whom David calls 'my Lord'. The question then arises, 'Who is David's Lord?' Who could be so great that David, the greatest king of Israel, could refer to Him as 'my Lord', a title with implications of deity? Clearly this Son of David, this future Messiah, is greater than David, has divine attributes, and is invited by God to sit at His right hand until all His enemies are subdued.

If we come to the point in life where we realize that Jesus Christ is Lord over all, God's risen, ascended, glorified King waiting to crush His enemies and bring in His everlasting kingdom, then suddenly all our other more minor questions dissolve, and Christ becomes all in all.

REFLECTION

What is the biggest question you are asking God in your life right now? Why is worshipping Jesus more important than that question?

The widow giving her two mites into the Temple treasury (vv. 41–44) offers a bit of light relief from Jesus' conflicts with religious leaders. The camera shifts subtly away from the subterfuge of the power brokers seeking Jesus' life, to this humble woman giving her all for God.

There is a message here about what matters to God. No doubt the Sanhedrin felt they were the important men in Israel, trying to rid Judaism of Christ's messianic pretensions. But Jesus' focus is not on the powerful, but on humble saints whom no one else notices.

Sitting near to where all the rich were clanging in their golden coins, the Lord draws special attention to this poor widow. She would probably have been dressed in black, with a shawl across her face, hurrying out of the Temple sanctuary before anyone noticed her seemingly puny offering. But Christ was delighting in her, so much so that He makes a point about her to His disciples.

'I tell you the truth, this poor widow has put more into the treasury than all the others' (v. 43). Clearly God is less interested in the amount that we give, than in how much it costs us to give. Remember King David bargaining over the threshing floor of Araunah the Jebusite so that he could build an altar (2 Sam. 24). Araunah was going to offer him the site for free, but David insisted, 'I will not sacrifice to the LORD…offerings that cost me nothing' (v. 24). What a great motto for a disciple of Christ.

Mark contrasts the humble, discreet widow with the ostentation of the teachers of the law who 'like to walk around in flowing robes…and have the most important seats in the synagogues' (vv. 38,39). Jesus hates religious showmanship, but delights in those who live for an audience of One, and give without out their left hand knowing what their right hand is doing. The highest seats in glory will be reserved for the quietest, most humble, most faithful disciples – 'the last will be first, and the first will be last' (Matt. 20:16).

Notice again how the person of Christ divides people. The Sanhedrin want to take His life, the widow is giving her whole life. She symbolizes the costly discipleship at the heart of Mark's Gospel. There are only really two responses to Christ – you want rid of Him, or you want to give your all to Him. There is no middle ground.

REFLECTION

Are you trying to create a middle ground in your commitment to Christ? Are you living for an audience of One?

To grasp this long and detailed passage, we need to understand how prophecy works. Jesus is following in the tradition of Old Testament prophets by predicting an event in the near future that is also a foretaste of a more distant event. Theologians call this 'telescoping'. Isaiah does this by predicting that a son would be born to a virgin (Isa. 7), as a sign to King Ahaz in his own day, but that prediction also serves as a pointer to the ultimate 'son of a virgin' who would be born to Mary in Bethlehem 700 years later.

Likewise in this passage, Jesus predicts the upcoming destruction of the Jewish Temple (v. 2), and the terrible days that would surround it (vv. 17–19), and that prediction serves as a springboard to describe the events that will surround the second coming of Christ. In AD 70, Roman soldiers marched into Jerusalem and laid waste to the Temple, forcing people to flee to the mountains as they killed men, women and children in a fearful bloodbath.

But Jesus clearly moves beyond the AD 70 destruction to describe what it will be like when 'the Son of Man [comes in] great power and glory' (v. 26). The New Testament is consistent in painting a picture of terrible times as we approach Christ's return, marked by deceivers (vv. 21,22), the persecution of Christians (v. 9), and the coming of Antichrist who will cause 'the abomination that causes desolation' (v. 14) – some kind of sacrilegious event, as the Antichrist wants to assume divine status himself (see 2 Thess. 2:3,4).

But we are promised that the terror of the tribulation will be followed by the victory of Christ's visible, personal return, when He gathers 'his elect from the four winds, from the ends of the earth to the ends of the heavens' (v. 27). Jesus doesn't tell us these things to alarm us, but so that we will be watchful (vv. 32–37). We do not know when Jesus will come, so we need to be busy about our Master's business, holy in our lifestyle, and diligent in prayer, so we will be ready for our Lord's return.

The great puritan Jonathan Edwards made a promise in his early days that he would try to live each day as though it were his last. If you were told that you had a week left to live before Jesus came through the clouds, what priorities would you change in your life? Hurry up, then, because you may not have a week...

REFLECTION

Do you believe that Jesus could return at any moment? What do you need to do to be ready?

It tells us something about Mark's priorities that he devotes fully a third of his Gospel to Jesus' Passion week in Jerusalem (chs. 11–16). In fact, one commentator suggested that Mark's Gospel is a Passion narrative with an extended introduction. That is probably taking it too far, but there is no doubt that Mark's central theme is to point us to God's Suffering Servant.

Those who suggest that Christ's incarnation is as important as His crucifixion, who say that the theme of 'God with us' equals the theme of 'Christ died for us', cannot look to Mark for support. Mark does not even mention Jesus' birth, but for several chapters now, he has given us the grand build-up to Calvary.

Christ did not come into our world simply to be with us. If that is all He had done, however remarkable the incarnation is, we would be heading to judgement. He came to build a bridge between sinful humanity and a holy God, on His own dead body. Nothing else about Christ's life matters quite as much as His death for sin, and glorious resurrection. Perhaps people want to take the focus elsewhere because sin and judgement aren't themes we like to talk about, but they form the heartbeat of biblical redemption.

So central is Jesus' death that Mark highlights the sacrificial act of a woman who anoints Jesus' body with perfume, 'to prepare for my burial' (v. 8). Her perfume was 'pure nard' (John 12:3), an expensive perfume, which she broke with abandon and poured on Christ's head. True discipleship is costly, because the Lord we worship is worthy of our very best. And sometimes we need to stand out from the crowd, even in church, to give Christ our all, when more cynical observers see wholehearted discipleship as too radical.

The beauty of her deed is set against the dark shadow of Judas agreeing with the religious leaders to betray Jesus. It is difficult to miss the importance of money in this emotive story. The woman is rebuked for recklessly spending on Christ, while Judas plots to betray the Son of God for money. How we use our money shows how much Jesus really means to us.

Mark also highlights how much the person of Christ divides people. You either want Him dead, or you want to give everything for Him. There are no 'in betweens' in Mark's Gospel. Christ remains the great dividing line in history. You can utterly reject Him, or you can give your all for Him. What you must not do is treat the controversial Christ half-heartedly.

REFLECTION

Why is Jesus' death and resurrection more important than anything else He did? Are you giving Him your all?

I have a 9-month-old son at home, and there comes that inevitable moment during the night when he will wake up and call out for us. That's when I need to make a decision. Will I go and comfort him, or will I ignore him and hope my wife goes and gets him? It is nice to be with my son and see his smiles, but I have to admit, it is so much easier to ignore him. And that's how many people treat Christ. It is so much easier to ignore Him. But this famous passage reminds us that we can't ignore Him

1. Because of His sovereignty. Jesus is in full control of the events that will lead up to His death. He seems to have supernatural knowledge as He directs His disciples to 'a man carrying a jar of water' (v. 13). That was an unusual sight because women usually carried water jars. But this man would direct them to the room where Jesus would share the Passover – a meal when He would explain in advance what His death would mean. He is in control. Not only so, but He predicts Peter's denial and Judas' treachery. Jesus is not the unfortunate victim of circumstance as He approaches the cross. He is fully aware that He is laying down His life for the sins of the world.

2. Because of His scrutiny. Jesus was able to read the deep inner motives of Judas, when the other disciples had no idea what was going on, and He even knew Peter better than Peter knew himself. Jesus is able to look behind the curtains of our hearts, and know our deepest, darkest motives. We are constantly under His scrutiny, like the seven churches of Revelation. Keep your heart pure and holy – remember Paul telling the Corinthians his conscience was clear, but that still did not free him from the judgement of the all-seeing Christ (1 Cor. 4:4).

3. Because of His sacrifice. Jesus used the Passover meal, centred round the lamb that was slaughtered to free Israel from slavery (Exod. 12:1–13), to explain His upcoming death. His blood would establish a 'new covenant' wherein God would forgive and accept His people, not on the basis of their ability to keep His moral law, but on Christ's substitutionary atonement for sin.

REFLECTION

What difference does it make to know that Jesus knows you through and through? Are you still trusting in the blood of the Lamb?

Jesus' fate was sealed not on a hill outside Jerusalem, but in a valley beneath it. It was sealed not with a betrayer's kiss, or a midnight arrest, but with a submission of the will. No one can take Christ's life from Him. He must lay it down. And now in this moment of moments, the God-man wrestles in His spirit with the crushing realities of Calvary.

It is not so much the thought of nails and thorns, or even mockery at the hands of priests and soldiers that leads to Jesus' troubled spirit in Gethsemane. It's the thought of 'the cup' (v. 36). He had lifted up a cup to His disciples as He instituted the communion meal, saying, 'This is the new covenant in My blood.' Now He asks His Father to relieve Him of 'the cup' of suffering.

'The cup' was an Old Testament motif pointing to the wrath of God, used in the context of exiles when God poured His wrath out on decadent, sinful Jerusalem by allowing Babylonian invaders to tear the holy city apart. Now Jesus realized that this cup of wrath was going to tear Him apart at Golgotha. This is what made him fall to the ground and pray (see v. 35). The most unbearable thought to the spotless Son of God was dying under the wrath of His Father, becoming all that is hideous to His Father's righteousness. Jesus' sheer manly courage is beyond words as He rouses His own soul to say, 'not what I will, but what you will' (v. 36).

Christ's rugged determination is in sharp contrast to the sleepy disciples, who are in no mood to battle with their wills. 'The spirit is willing, but the body is weak' (v. 38). Every time we struggle to pray, or fight temptation, we need to fix our eyes on Christ's sheer resolve. It was not His divine power that got Him through Gethsemane, but His love for His Father, and for me and you.

The arrest scene (vv. 43–52) contains the repeated word in Greek, 'take hold of' or 'seize' (vv. 45,46,48). Soldiers are only able to 'take hold of' Jesus, because He has 'taken hold of' His own soul. The unnamed naked deserter (v. 52) is deliberately anonymous so we can put our own names here. We are forced to examine our own willingness to abandon Jesus when the going gets tough.

REFLECTION

Compare Jesus' willingness to bend His will to the Father to your own. How much are you prepared to endure to obey God?

You may not know the name Marcia Clark, but she was the prosecution lawyer during the infamous O.J. Simpson trial. Prior to prosecuting Simpson, Marcia Clark had won 19 of her 20 cases and was considered an outstanding legal talent. Following the trial she gave up legal work, feeling exhausted and exposed by the whole thing. She said she felt on trial herself, as wall-to-wall news coverage commented on everything from her prosecuting style to her hairstyle.

And this passage also makes us ask, 'Who is really on trial?' Ostensibly it's Jesus, bound and chained. But Mark also seems to place the spotlight on the motives of the Sanhedrin who are trying Him, and on Peter who is denying Him.

The Sanhedrin want rid of Jesus, plain and simple. While proclaiming themselves staunch defenders of the law, they cobble together an illegal trial that should never have taken place during the night. And when Jesus declares Himself the Son of Man, a claim to deity, the high priest does not ask for any evidence or proof. He tears his robes in protest and passes swift sentence, unprepared to countenance that Jesus might be the God He claimed to be. And as we share the gospel today, we must remember that many people have their minds totally closed. As the respected scientist Richard Lewontin said, 'we cannot allow a Divine Foot in the door'.

As for Jesus, His silence under pressure is deafening. To all the lies and the vindictiveness of the Sanhedrin, Jesus replies not a word. He absorbs it all without any thought of vengeance, entrusting His way to God, and knowing that He has been chosen as 'a lamb for the slaughter'. I wonder if we can respond with such restraint when lies and gossip are being spread about us.

Peter's faith famously cracks under pressure. He warms himself by a fire (v. 54), a symbol of the fiery trial he is passing through. And while Peter's Lord is being beaten upstairs, Peter denies even knowing Him, under pressure from a mere servant girl.

But before we are too hard on Peter, at least he was there. All the other disciples had run for their lives. Peter put himself in the place to fail, and ironically his failure was the making of a man who preached with gusto at Pentecost, and later died as a courageous martyr. Are you attempting enough for Christ to fail Him?

REFLECTION

How do you respond when your faith is put under pressure? Who do you relate to most – Jesus, Peter, or the Sanhedrin?

Twice in this chapter Mark records that Pilate was amazed by Jesus. He was amazed by Jesus' silence in front of His accusers (v. 5), and by Jesus' death (v. 44). Silence and death aren't the kind of things that normally amaze us about people. They are signs of weakness. But Mark wants to show us that the Son of God is amazing, precisely because of His weakness. Mark tells us Jesus is amazing

1. In His submission. Several times in the previous chapter we are told that Jesus was 'handed over'. He is always the object, never the subject. Handed over by Judas, by soldiers, by priests, and here by Pilate. He stands silent and in chains. However, several times in chapter 15 Jesus is called 'King'. How can He be King and yet be handed over, bound, mocked, beaten and crucified? Jesus is submitting to God's will, to redeem a lost humanity. That's what makes Him kingly. What is God calling you to submit to in your life? Submission is an unpopular word on earth, but a glorious word in heaven.

2. In His substitution. The crowd shout out for the guilty Barabbas to be released while the innocent Christ is crucified. Mark is telling us here the deeper meaning behind Jesus' death. Isaiah 53 teaches us that substitution is at the heartbeat of redemption. Christ, the innocent one, died in the place of you and me, the guilty ones: 'he was pierced for our transgressions'

(Isa. 53:5). He bore the wrath I deserve, in His body on the tree.

3. In His suffering. The Gospels downplay Jesus' physical suffering. Verse 15 simply says, 'He [Pilate] had Jesus flogged, and handed him over to be crucified.' Flogging or scourging meant whipping a prisoner's back with a whip lined with pieces of metal and bone. The whip opened the flesh, and many prisoners were known to die from scourging alone. Christ's sufferings were extreme and grotesque. Isaiah 52:14 suggests He was almost unrecognizable as a human being. And all of that for you and me!

The German philosopher Nietzsche hated Christianity because of its weakness. He said the pitiful Christ was 'mankind's greatest misfortune'. But for those who believe, Jesus is precious, precisely because of His weakness. His submission, substitution and suffering declare in bold letters 'God is love'.

REFLECTION

Remind yourself today of what Christ endured to save you from sin. How does this passage change your view of your own weaknesses?

It is difficult for us to imagine how appalling crucifixion was in the ancient world. We dignify the cross as an item of jewellery, but crucifixion was such a horror in the first century you could not even mention it in polite conversation. A famous piece of graffiti was discovered in second-century Corinth, picturing a man bowing before a crucified victim. The crucified victim had a donkey's head, showing the scorn and mockery which surrounded crucifixion. Underneath the caption reads 'Alexamenos worships his God'.

Paul later said that the notion of crucifixion was a 'stumbling block to Jews and foolishness to Gentiles' (1 Cor. 1:23). Mark does not try to hide the 'shame' of crucifixion. The soldiers mock Christ, putting a purple robe and crown of thorns on Him. But there is irony here, because what they say in mockery is true at a deeper level than any can perceive – He really is 'king of the Jews' (v. 18).

Nor does Mark hide the fact that Jesus was too weak to carry His cross, or that as He hung naked, His earthly clothes were the focus of a betting game, or that those who passed by 'hurled insults at him, shaking their heads' (v. 29), mocking Him for His inability to save Himself, let alone the world. Even those crucified with Him mocked the broken Jesus.

Mark does nothing to cover over the shame of Jesus' crucifixion. Why not? Why, when Mark clearly wants us to see Jesus as King, does he not downplay the shame? Probably because Christ's kingship is best seen by His taking on the brokenness and degradation of the world. He became a picture of all the damage sin causes – the alienation and disgrace of 'everyman'. The crown of thorns itself speaks of the futility that entered the world when God cursed the ground, and caused fruitless painful thorns to grow.

Jesus is here taking on the mantle of the righteous sufferer from the Psalms. All that He endures, from the mockery of Gentiles, to the division of His clothes, to the religious leaders throwing insults – all of these were prophesied in the Psalms. Christ is God's anointed King who would carry the shame of the world on His shoulders, just as it was written.

Our heroes today are rebellious, mega-wealthy, cavalier hedonists. Those our world worships are empty shells. But here is God's Christ literally carrying the pain of the world on His back. Behind the blood, shame and mockery, you find a most beautiful Lord who absorbed the world's evil in His own body. That's what makes Him King of kings.

REFLECTION

Are you ashamed of Jesus in any way? To what extent have you faced shame in following Him?

The climax of Mark's Gospel comes with the centurion's cry, 'Surely this man was the Son of God!' (v. 39). Remember how Mark opened his Gospel: 'the beginning of the gospel about Jesus Christ, the Son of God' (1:1). Mark is out to prove that Jesus is the Son of God, and ironically it is a Gentile 'outsider', a Roman soldier crucifying Him, who makes the great confession as a crescendo to the whole book.

It is not until His death that Christ's Son of God status is fully revealed. Halfway through the Gospel, Peter makes a declaration that is partially true, 'You are the Christ' (Mark 8:29), but Peter's Christ was a blurry image which did not include suffering and death. Mark has been trying to tell us all the way through, by pointing to the cross from early on in the Gospel, and by spending a third of his Gospel on the last week of Jesus' life, that who Christ really is can only be seen at the cross.

Through His death, a power is unleashed from heaven that rips the Temple curtain, and opens the way for humanity to enter God's presence again. The offence of our sin which separated us from God is wiped away by Jesus' sacrifice, and we can now draw 'within the veil' – what a privilege we have every time we pray 'in Jesus' name'.

But access into the Holy of Holies is only granted for us, because it was denied to Christ. 'Eloi, eloi, lama sabachthani' (v. 34). At key moments, Mark retains Jesus' original Aramaic words to reflect the emotion of the utterance. In Gethsemane, Jesus calls God His 'Abba' Father. When He is raising Jairus' daughter, he keeps the phrase 'Talitha koum', meaning 'Little girl, get up'.

The effect is not only to give an eyewitness touch of the real words Jesus uttered, but also to reflect the heightened passion of the moment. Jesus, who had cried out in Gethsemane with fervour to His 'Abba' Father, now cries out with utter desolation 'My God, where are You?' He cannot call God 'Father', because for the first and only time in eternity there is a rupture in the Trinity, as the Father cannot look on our sin-bearer. Here we enter a holy mystery...

But it is Jesus' desolation that brings us salvation; Jesus' banishment that gives us access. Salvation is free for the receiver, but extremely costly for the Saviour.

REFLECTION

Meditate on the cost of your salvation. 'Love so amazing, so divine, Demands my soul, my life, my all.'[2]

Characteristically for Mark, he closes his gospel with a sandwich. The boldness of Joseph in asking for Jesus' body is set in contrast with the doubt and fear of the women. The women were watching the cross 'from a distance', (vv. 40,41), and when they hear the angels announcing that Jesus has risen, 'Trembling and bewildered, the women went out and fled from the tomb. They said nothing to anyone, because they were afraid' (16:8).

In between, Joseph makes his move, 'Joseph of Arimathea, a prominent member of the Council...went boldly to Pilate and asked for Jesus' body' (v. 43). His courage is remarkable as he was a well-known member of the Sanhedrin whose treachery had crucified Christ. In days to come, Joseph would no doubt face some awkward questions for associating himself so openly with a 'blasphemer' like Jesus.

Let's remember that this was a time when disciples were locking themselves away in fear of the Jewish leadership. But Joseph, very publicly, and in line with prophecy (Isa. 53:9), takes Jesus' broken body down from the cross, wraps it carefully in expensive linen, and places it in a new tomb.

Mark is asking us a penetrating question at the end of his gospel – which type of disciple are we? Are we the fearful, distant type who doesn't say anything about Christ to anyone be-cause we are concerned how people might react? Or are we the Joseph kind, taking our courage in both hands, and publicly associating with the contro-versial Christ, no matter what the cost – giving ourselves and our money (new tombs were expensive, like the wom-an's perfume in ch. 14) to honour Jesus in a world that wants to see Him dead?

You will notice in your Bible that the Gospel of Mark contains verses 9 to 20 in some of its ancient manuscripts. But the most reliable and earliest manuscripts stop at verse 8. You could see why an overzealous scribe might have felt that you cannot finish a gospel with a note of trembling and bewildered women leaving a tomb (16:8).

Surely we need more triumph, more preaching the gospel across the globe, more tongues-speaking and being able to drink deadly poison without being harmed (vv. 17,18). But that ending would spoil the challenge Mark really wanted to leave us with. Much of our discipleship is not victorious – it is of the trembling and bewildered type. But Jesus is still beckoning to us doubters to leave everything, to take up our cross and follow Him.

REFERENCES

[1] A.W. Tozer, *The Knowledge of the Holy* (Milton Keynes: Authentic Media, 2005).

[2] 'When I Survey the Wondrous Cross' by Isaac Watts 1674–1748.

MORE IN THIS SERIES

ROMANS: Momentous News *By David Cook*
ISBN: 978-1-906173-24-1

DANIEL: Far From Home *By Justin Mote*
ISBN: 978-1-906173-68-5

1 THESSALONIANS: Living for Jesus *By Julia Marsden*
ISBN: 978-1-906173-67-8

10 Publishing
a division of 10ofthose.com

To place an order call: **0844 879 3243** email: **sales@10ofthose.com**
or order online: **www.10ofthose.com**

10Publishing is the publishing house of 10ofThose.
It is committed to producing quality Christian
resources that are biblical and accessible.

www.10ofthose.com is our online retail arm selling
thousands of quality books at discounted prices.
We also service many church bookstalls
and can help your church to set up a bookstall.
Single and bulk purchases welcome.

For information contact: sales@10ofthose.com
or check out our website: www.10ofthose.com